Palace Princesses

Victoria

Contents

Elizabeths to the right, Marys to the left, if you please.

Born a princess

Since Norman times, it's been usual for a king to pass the crown to his eldest son. If he has no sons, his eldest daughter becomes queen. Unfair? It's still the law today.

Matilda rules OK!

Princess Matilda was born in 1102, the daughter of Henry I. When Matilda's older brother William was drowned at sea, she became heir to the throne. There had never been a queen of England before, so Henry had to make his powerful barons promise that Matilda would rule after him.

Matilda had a fiery temper. She even fell out with the people on her side.

In 1140, Stephen tried to hold court at the Tower of London. But Matilda was causing such trouble, his barons were afraid to join him.

Broken promises

When Henry died, the barons broke their promise. They offered the throne to Matilda's easy-going cousin Stephen instead. Matilda was FURIOUS! For nearly 20 years Matilda and Stephen battled for the crown. Eventually, Matilda's supporters gave up and she retreated to France. Her son Henry took up the fight and Stephen agreed that he would be the next king. **Result!**

Henry VIII was desperate for a son to rule after him. When his second wife, Anne Boleyn, gave birth to a daughter Henry was FUMING.

Rags to riches

Can you become a princess even if your father isn't a king? Yes you can! You can try and kiss a frog like the princess in *The Frog Prince*. Or you can marry a prince like Lady Diana Spencer did. She married Prince Charles and became Diana, Princess of Wales.

Have your say

If you were a princess... Would you want the law changed so that princes and princesses would have equal rights to the throne?

Lady Diana Spencer aged 5.

The Prince and Princess of Wales on their wedding day, July 1981.

Bah! a girl! No wrestling No riding No rough stuff

Although the christening of Henry's daughter went ahead, all the jousts (mock fights on horseback) were cancelled.

All jousts cancelled

3

A fairy-tale palace?

Princesses live in palaces – but what's it like to live in one? Loads of servants to tidy your room? Snacks whenever you want? A huge four-poster bed? Sometimes – but not always.

Kensington Palace

In 1819, Princess Victoria was born in Kensington Palace. Her father died nine months later. Her mother, the Duchess of Kent, was penniless because her husband had died owing loads of money. For the first 18 years Victoria and her mother lived in ground floor rooms that she described as 'dreadfully dull, dark and gloomy'. What's more the palace was infested with what Victoria described as 'our Kensington friends':

big black beetles!

I want my own room!

Life at Kensington Palace was lonely and boring for young Victoria. She had to spend all her time with adults. Victoria even had to sleep in the same room as her mother until she was 18!

Gross!

Kensington Palace.

Princess Victoria's life wasn't all gloomy. She was given this carriage with two Shetland ponies for her seventh birthday.

In Tudor times, Princess Mary stayed at Hampton Court Palace. Workmen had to make her rooms bigger to fit in all her ladies-in-waiting, servants and hangers-on...

An upgrade

When it became clear that one day Victoria would become queen, her mother demanded grander rooms. The old State Apartments in Kensington Palace were converted into new apartments for Victoria and her mother. Victoria was delighted and described her new sitting room as 'very prettily furnished'.

The doll's house at Kew House.

Princess Victoria aged 14. By now, Victoria knew that she would become queen.

A mini palace

The daughters of George III, who lived in Kew Palace, made furniture for this beautiful doll's house. When they got too old for it they gave it to the children of the captain of the royal yacht.

...but it was still a bit of a tight squeeze!

School rules

Princesses don't have to learn lessons. Right? Wrong! In the past, the cleverest tutors taught princesses at home. These days, they are more likely to go to an expensive boarding school.

Princess Elizabeth, Queen Charlotte's artistic daughter, was taught how to make these silhouettes using scissors, paper and paint.

Lessons at Kew Palace

In the 1700s, princesses were usually taught to be dutiful and to look pretty. But Queen Charlotte, the wife of George III, believed her six daughters should be as well educated as her nine sons. She employed famous artists and musicians to teach her princesses how to draw and to play musical instruments.

Charlotte Finch probably used these counters to teach the alphabet.

Lady Charlotte Finch was governess to Queen Charlotte's children.

Princess Sophia, Queen Charlotte's fifth daughter, builds a house of cards.

fab schooly facts

- ☆ Princess Alexandra, our Queen's cousin, was the first British princess to go to an ordinary school.
- ☆ Princess Victoria's tutors said her handwriting was RUBBISH!
- ☆ Princess Elizabeth, Henry VIII's daughter, could read and write in five different languages.

Lessons at Kensington Palace

Princess Victoria had lessons six days a week. They lasted from 9.30am to 11.30am, followed by a break, a walk and lunch at 1pm. From 3pm to 5pm there were more lessons and then from 5pm to 6pm she learnt poetry by heart. **PHEW!**

The Reverend Davys arranged Victoria's lessons. He also taught her religious knowledge, history and geography. Each Thursday she had a dancing lesson which she loved, and on Fridays she was taught music.

This picture of Princess Victoria sketching was painted by Robert Westall, her art teacher.

Victoria's strict timetable was planned by Sir John Conroy, chief adviser to her mother. It was called the Kensington System.

So long, Sir John

Victoria hated Sir John. She got her revenge when she became queen. He demanded grand titles, power and a pension - but she said **No Way!** and sent him packing.

Pets for princesses

In the Middle Ages, kings and princes were often presented with lions, bears and elephants. Queens and princesses were given exotic birds. Nowadays, princesses are more likely to be given pets as birthday presents.

Princess Victoria drew this picture of Dash, her *beloved* spaniel. She liked to dress him up in a red jacket and *blue* trousers!

Princess Mary, Sophie and Amelia, George III's three youngest daughters play happily with their dogs. Can you name the breed of dogs?

Princess Elizabeth (Windsor) with her pet corgi, Dookie.

When Princess Anne (Windsor) was 4, she was given a baby brown bear called Nikki. It was given to London Zoo.

The daughters of George III kept pet kangaroos at Kew which bred like mad. The babies were given away to people at court.

5 fab pet facts

☆ All royal corgis are descended from Princess Elizabeth's pet corgi, Susan.
☆ 'Dookie' is an old slang word for poo!
☆ Princess Victoria's favourite pony was called Rosy.
☆ The first thing Victoria did after her coronation was to give Dash a bath!
☆ Princess Alexandra of Denmark taught her parrot Cocky to say 'God save the Queen'.

A passion for fashion

Princesses' clothes are usually the best money can buy. Some princesses become fashion icons and their style is copied by millions of women all over the world.

Designer labels

Princess Diana was one of the most photographed women – EVER. When she attended special events, she usually wore dresses designed by top British designers to support the British fashion industry. She knew that what she wore would always be front page news in newspapers and magazines.

This photograph shows Princess Diana wearing the dress to a State Banquet in Japan.

for Princess Diana

style 15/54

This sketch, by designer Zandra Rhodes, is for a dress for an official visit to Japan.

Diana wore this dark blue velvet dress to a State Dinner in the USA in 1985. She danced with John Travolta, a famous film star.

Anne of Cleves, Henry VIII's fourth wife was not a fashion icon.

Copy cat

People copied the clothes of young princesses too. This is what one young girl said about growing up at the same time as Princesses Elizabeth and Margaret in the Second World War.

> *Growing up in the war, we had no sort of idols, pop groups or singers. We looked up to the little princesses and if they wore a frilly dress, our mothers gave us a frilly dress. If they wore twinsets, my Mum would knit me a twinset.*

This dress was designed in the style of Grace Kelly, a famous film star who also married a prince.

Princess Elizabeth aged 11 and Princess Margaret aged 7.

What a pong

Anne's clothes were described as 'monstrous'. It was said that she was a bit smelly too!

Have your say

If you were a princess... What would you wear to: A very grand ball? To open a hospital? To go to the gym?

Get the look!

Most princesses like to wear the latest make-up and hairstyles. Today, they buy ready-made cosmetics and go to posh hairdressers. How did they manage in the past?

Loads of clothes

Princesses Anne, Amelia and Caroline were brought up in Kensington Palace by their grandfather, George I. They seem to have led a rather boring life. BUT they had loads of lovely clothes and each had 192 pairs of gloves a year and a new pair of shoes **every week!**

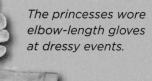

The princesses wore shoes like this. This one is made of leather and silk satin and decorated with silver-gilt braid and embroidery.

Princesses Anne, Amelia and Caroline in 1721.

Shoes and gloves

Why did princesses need so many shoes and gloves? Two hundred and fifty years ago, expensive shoes were often made of delicate materials such as silk. Imagine what they looked like after a walk in the palace gardens! Gloves made of fine leather tore easily and were difficult to clean. Princesses couldn't be seen dead with scruffy shoes or gloves so they were thrown away.

The princesses wore elbow-length gloves at dressy events.

Make-up and makeovers

In the early 1700s, fashionable ladies liked to look like delicate china dolls. They whitened their faces with powder, pencilled their eyebrows and wore plenty of rouge (blusher). Make-up was made from all sorts of ingredients such as flower petals, melon and honey, mixed with dew and egg white. Lipstick was made of plaster and red dye.

Spots and pimples

Some make-up contained poisonous ingredients that damaged the skin. The deadly disease smallpox, a common illness then, left survivors with ugly pock marks. So small, shaped black patches made to cover scars became very popular.

This gorgeous perfume bottle is the type that princesses would have used.

This patch box belonged to Queen Mary II.

Two hundred years ago, ladies were encouraged to wash their faces with rosemary boiled in white wine – and drink any left over as a cure for 'stinking breath'!

The grand birthday ball

Do you remind friends and family when your birthday is due? The royal family don't need to. Their birthdays are announced in newspapers and posted on the web, and celebrated in style!

The birthday balls

Every year, King George III and Queen Charlotte each held a grand ball on their birthdays. Their daughters, Princesses Charlotte, Augusta, Elizabeth, Mary, Amelia and Sophia, got to choose the silk for new dresses! All the stars of the day came dressed in the latest designer fashion to gawp and gossip. So it was very important that their dresses were more expensive and fashionable than anyone else's.

This picture from The New Lady's Magazine *shows Prince George dancing with Princess Charlotte at the Queen's birthday ball, 1786.*

Silk samples were sent to the princesses. They chose one to be made up into a ball dress.

Princess Augusta wore this dress to the King's birthday ball in 1799.

Go Beatrice!

Princess Beatrice's 18th birthday was extra special because she was born on the eighth day of the eighth month in 1988!

Fancy dress

Beatrice celebrated in style with a ball for 500 guests at Windsor Castle. Famous celebrities mixed with princes and princesses and everyone rocked up in fancy dress. The theme? The year 1888, when Beatrice's great-great-great-grandmother, Queen Victoria, was on the throne.

Princess Beatrice, (next to her father) and her family dressed in Victorian fancy dress.

Ooh! you are a dumpling

In the 1760s, women's waists had to be made impossibly small with tightly laced corsets to balance the wide hips of their fashionable ball dresses.

These enormous dresses had petticoats (underskirts) worn over huge side hoops made of cane and whale bone. Ladies took up a great deal of space when they moved.

OY!

Ladies first

me first

Wicked stepmothers

Fairy tales are full of jealous stepmothers. In *Snow White*, the wicked queen plots against her beautiful young stepdaughter. And it happened in real life too!

Princess Mary.

Anne Boleyn had magnificent apartments at Hampton Court. Mary lived miles away from court.

Anne Boleyn, Henry VIII's second wife.

The new queen

Anne Boleyn, Henry VIII's second wife was madly jealous of her stepdaughter, Princess Mary. And when Anne gave birth to a baby girl named Princess Elizabeth, things got worse.

Princess Mary was the daughter of Henry VIII and his first wife Katherine of Aragon. Henry was desperate for a son to rule after him. So, when Katherine got too old to have more children, Henry divorced her and married Anne Boleyn.

Plots and insults

Anne Boleyn persuaded Henry that Mary wasn't a princess because Katherine was no longer queen! Then Anne boasted that she would employ Mary as a lady's maid to the new baby. **WHAT AN INSULT!**

Mary fights back

But Mary was a fighter! On one occasion she was invited to admire baby Elizabeth. But she refused saying there was only one princess **AND THAT WAS HER!**

Anne was furious. She gave orders that if Mary used the banned title of 'Princess' again she would be punished! What's more, Anne knew that Henry had a soft spot for his daughter and might feel sorry for her. So when he visited the palaces where Mary was staying, Anne made sure they didn't meet. **Booo!**

This picture shows Henry VIII proudly introducing Anne Boleyn to court. It was painted by William Hogarth, over 200 years later.

When Anne Boleyn failed to produce a son she got nervous. She asked a fortune-teller what was going to happen. The fortune-teller told her that she would never have another baby as long as Katherine and Mary were alive! **Scary!!!**

How Anne must have hated Mary when it proved to be true!

Princesses in prison

Being a princess could be dangerous. In the past, some princesses were plotted against, held hostage, imprisoned or even threatened with execution!

A suspicious sister

In 1554, Mary I, a Catholic, was Queen of England. Mary thought her sister, Princess Elizabeth, who was a Protestant, was plotting against her. So she ordered her to be imprisoned in the Tower of London. Elizabeth wrote to Mary asking if she could see her and explain that she was innocent. But the Queen refused her request.

Traitors' Gate.

Mary I.

To the Tower!

The next day Elizabeth was arrested and secretly taken to the Tower by barge. Most prisoners arrived through Traitors' Gate. But Elizabeth was a royal princess so she probably came up the Queen's Steps – but no one knows for sure.

The Tower was prison to another princess too. In 1140, Princess Constance arrived from France to marry Eustace, the son of King Stephen. At that time, Stephen was fighting Matilda for the crown.

Princess Elizabeth

Living in fear

Mary kept Elizabeth in the Tower for two months. Imagine how she felt knowing that her mother, Anne Boleyn, had been executed near the rooms where she was imprisoned. And, that she herself, also might be beheaded! **Seriously scary!**

Mary couldn't prove anything against Elizabeth so she sent her to live miles away from court. But the danger wasn't over. Elizabeth knew that she could be re-arrested at any time. Then, in 1558, Mary died and Elizabeth became queen.
PHEW!

This ring belonged to Princess Elizabeth. It contains a picture of her mother Anne Boleyn.

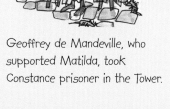

Geoffrey de Mandeville, who supported Matilda, took Constance prisoner in the Tower.

Stephen persuaded Geoffrey to release Constance. In return, the King made Geoffrey an earl.

Constance married Eustace. But later, Stephen punished Geoffrey by taking all his castles away.

Tear-jerkers

The life of a princess isn't always what it's cracked up to be. Especially when your beloved father is going to be beheaded!

Sentenced to death

Princess Elizabeth was the daughter of Charles I. In 1649, Charles was sentenced to death because he had fought a war against his parliament and lost.

Charles was beheaded outside the Banqueting House, in London's Whitehall.

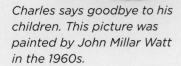

Charles says goodbye to his children. This picture was painted by John Millar Watt in the 1960s.

Goodbye daddy...

The night before his execution, 13-year-old Elizabeth and her 9-year-old brother Henry visited the King in Whitehall Palace. Elizabeth cried so much her father wasn't sure that she had heard his final words. But after she left, Elizabeth wrote down what he had said.

What the King said

The King told her that he was glad to see her and that she shouldn't cry. He was going to die for the things he believed in so he had forgiven his enemies. He said that Elizabeth, her mother, brothers and sisters should forgive them – but not to trust them!

A sad ending

After Charles's execution, no one knew what to do with Elizabeth and Henry because the rest of the family were living in the Netherlands. Finally, they were moved to Carisbrooke Castle on the Isle of Wight. Shortly after, Elizabeth caught pneumonia and died. She was 15.

Princess Elizabeth was found dead in her room. This picture was made much later, in Victorian times.

Princess Victoria's dolls dressed as the stars of ballets and operas she saw in London.

No friends

Princess Victoria (later Queen Victoria) wasn't allowed to have friends of her own age. So she invented a make-believe world around a small army of wooden dolls. She dressed them as people she admired such as famous ballerinas, actresses and opera singers. She even gave her dolls names, made up stories and played games with them.

Victoria's only real friend was Princess Feodora, her half-sister who was 12 years older. When Victoria was 9, Feodora married a German prince and went to live in Germany. Afterwards Victoria missed her half-sister terribly.

Princesses just wanna have

Do princesses really get fab presents, meet cool celebrities, wear beautiful clothes, go to the best places and have rock 'n' roll lifestyles?

Yes, they do!

When she was young her family described her as 'naughty but fun'.

Princess Margaret was the younger sister of our present Queen.

She loved clothes and wore all the latest fashions.

fun

She married Antony Armstrong-Jones, a trendy photographer and lived in Kensington Palace.

Her friends included celebrities, film stars and pop stars of the day.

4 fab pressies for princesses

✸ A Caribbean island given to Princess Margaret by her best friend.

✸ A brooch in the shape of a bee, with diamond-studded wings and ruby eyes, given to Margaret by her mother in 1945.

✸ A NEW pony called 'Greylight' given to Princess Margaret.

✸ GORGEOUS dolls dressed in designer clothes presented to Princesses Elizabeth and Margaret by the children of France.

Princesses with a purpose

In the past, princesses were thought to be mainly useful for marrying off to foreign princes and kings. In that way, kings could become more powerful. Today it's a very different story...

Princess Elizabeth learns how to strip down an engine.

Princess Elizabeth and her sister Princess Margaret, broadcast a message on the radio to cheer up children during the war.

Princesses at war

Our present Queen was a teenager during the Second World War. When she was 16 in 1945, she joined the army's Auxiliary Territorial Service. She learnt how to drive army vehicles and repair engines. According to her nanny, Princess Elizabeth was really proud of her uniform!

NAFF OFF!

Princess Anne is a world-class horsewoman. She doesn't mind falling off or getting muddy. Neither is she afraid of speaking her mind. She once told some photographers to 'Naff off'!

Land mines

Princess Diana visited Angola, in Africa, after war there had ended. She spent time with children who had lost limbs through land mine injuries. The pictures shown on television all over the world highlighted the terrible injures caused by land mines.

Princess Diana in Angola.

Princesses Bamba and Catherine Duleep Singh.

Votes for princesses!

In 1898 Princesses Bamba, Catherine and Sophia, daughters of Maharaja Duleep Singh, were granted a house near Hampton Court Palace by Queen Victoria. Their father was a good friend of the Queen and had brought his family to live in England. At that time, women weren't allowed to vote. Bamba and Catherine became 'suffragettes', the name for those who fought for women's right to vote.

The suffragettes tried to get attention by interrupting speeches in parliament, setting fire to buildings and even chaining themselves to the railings of Buckingham Palace. Imagine what the princesses living inside felt about that!

Life in a doll's house

Kew is the smallest royal palace. In the late 1700s, George III and his wife Queen Charlotte escaped the stuffy court life in London at weekends and lived in the countryside at Kew.

We want to go out!

Princesses Charlotte, Augusta, Elizabeth, Mary, Sophia and Amelia were the daughters of George III. The King was especially fond of them. In fact, he loved them so much he didn't want them to get married! But, as the princesses grew up, they longed to have their own homes and families.

Kew Palace.

They became desperate to get away from Queen Charlotte who wouldn't even let them choose their own clothes! While the princesses had to read 'good' books and spend hours doing embroidery, their nine brothers were allowed much more freedom.

How unfair is that !

King George III and Queen Charlotte and their six eldest children.

Things get worse

Things got worse in 1789 when the King became seriously ill with a rare disease. He was moved to Kew. George recovered, but his illness came back. Augusta, Elizabeth, Mary, Sophia and Amelia had to stay at Kew to look after the Queen who couldn't cope.

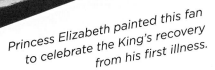

Princess Elizabeth painted this fan to celebrate the King's recovery from his first illness.

Elizabeth was the most artistic princess. She decorated the Picnic Room in the Queen's cottage at Kew.

Disappointed princesses

Princess Charlotte married but her only daughter died stillborn. Augusta never married. Sophia didn't marry but she had a baby in secret. Elizabeth and Mary married too late to have children. Amelia was forbidden to marry the man she loved and died of tuberculosis aged 27.

YAHOO! It's mine

When Kew Palace was redecorated in 1804, Princess Elizabeth bagged the best room for herself. She had an expensive new bed shaped like an ancient Greek couch covered in yellow and red fabric.

Sparklers!

Royal jewels are designed to send out serious messages – look how rich and powerful our country is! So jewellery is passed down the royal family from one generation to another. Imagine inheriting an Aladdin's cave full of gems as big as hen's eggs!

When Prince Albert became engaged to Victoria he gave her this brooch which he designed himself.

Princess Elizabeth, the daughter of King James I, wears jewels in her hair and round her neck. Even her dress is sprinkled with rubies and diamonds.

Princess Alexandra was the wife of Queen Victoria's eldest son, Bertie. She liked to wear loads of pearl necklaces to disguise a scar on her neck.

Princess Elizabeth and Princess Margaret's coronets were made for the coronation of their father, George VI. The jewels that the King and Queen wear here are Crown Jewels. That means they belong to the country, not to the royal family.

Princess Diana wears a tiara given to her by the Queen. Prince Charles gave her the necklace when Prince William was born.

B fab sparklers

☆ The most valuable diamond brooch in the world was inherited by Princess Elizabeth when she became queen.

☆ Princess Diana had very little jewellery before she married Prince Charles. Her father is supposed to have given her an empty jewel box – for Prince Charles to fill up!

☆ For her wedding, Princess Margaret wore a large diamond tiara. It was specially chosen to make her look taller.

Married off!

Kings often arranged marriages for their daughters when they were very young and couldn't say 'no'! But some princesses were lucky and got to choose their husbands.

True love

In 1836, when Princess Victoria was 16, Prince Ernest and Prince Albert arrived from Germany. Her mother thought they would make good husbands. Luckily Victoria liked them both, especially Albert. Her diary is full of tales of late nights, parties and balls. By the time they left, Victoria had decided she would marry Albert.

Three years later Victoria asked Albert to marry her. Although men usually proposed, Victoria knew Albert would never ask her because by then she was Queen of England and the most important woman in the world at that time.

Victoria and Albert.

What's the goss?

When Princess Elizabeth married Prince Philip in 1947, the Second World War had just ended. Gossip spread that the silk used to make her wedding dress came from Japan or Italy – Britain's enemies in the war. Fortunately, the silk was found to have come from Scotland.

Henry VIII's younger sister, Princess Mary, was very pretty. When she was 19, Henry married her off to King Louis XII of France who was sick, toothless and three times her age. Gross!

Mary only agreed to marry Louis after Henry promised that next time she could marry whoever she wanted.

The wedding

Victoria designed her own wedding dress and the dresses of her 12 bridesmaids.

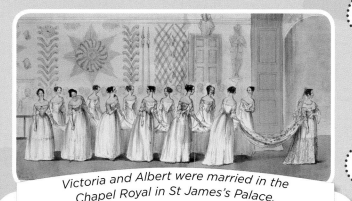

Victoria and Albert were married in the Chapel Royal in St James's Palace.

Victoria wore a wreath of orange blossom on her wedding day.

Lace made in Devon.

Her dress was made of silk satin woven in London.

Happy ever after?

Victoria and Albert had nine children and a very happy family life. Sadly, Prince Albert died unexpectedly aged 42. The Queen was overcome with grief and spent the rest of her life in mourning.

When Louis died two months later, Mary married Henry's best friend Charles Brandon, Duke of Suffolk – but without the King's permission! Henry was FURIOUS! Charles thought he would lose his head. But eventually the couple were forgiven.

Becoming queen

England has had six princesses who became queen:
Mary I, Elizabeth I, Mary II (who reigned with William III),
Anne, Victoria and Elizabeth II.

A princess becomes queen

Princess Elizabeth was on safari when she heard she was queen! In 1952, her father King George VI became ill and he had to cancel a grand tour of the Commonwealth. Princess Elizabeth and her husband Prince Philip went instead.

While she was in South Africa, the King died. He had no sons, so Elizabeth became queen.

Princess Elizabeth on her way to her father's funeral.

Queen Elizabeth II

The coronation of Queen Elizabeth II took place in Westminster Abbey. People were overjoyed to forget the dark days of the Second World War and look forward to a new beginning with a beautiful young queen. Over a million people came to London to see the decorations and the coronation procession. The Prime Minister, Winston Churchill, even ruled that sweets were no longer rationed.

Hooray!

The Queen travelled to Westminster Abbey in the gold coach built for George III for his coronation.

We saw it on the telly!

When the news announced that the coronation was to be televised for the first time, thousands of people rushed out to buy a TV set. Twenty-seven million watched in Britain alone. Millions more around the world watched it on television or listened to the coronation on the radio.

Elizabeth II was only 25 when she became queen.

Two little girls watch the coronation on their new TV set.

While Queen Elizabeth was in New Zealand on her grand tour of the Commonwealth, a loyal sheep farmer dyed his sheep red, white and blue. He herded his animals close to the track so that the Queen would see them as she passed in the royal train.

B fab queenly facts

☆ Henry VIII's eldest daughter Mary seized the throne from Lady Jane Grey. Then Mary had her beheaded!

☆ Mary's sister, Princess Elizabeth, was under the threat of death before she became queen.

☆ Princess Victoria was woken up at 6am in Kensington Palace to be told she was queen. She met her chief ministers in her nightie!

33

The princess parade

Look at this chart to find the princesses featured in this book.

1066-1154
The Normans

Matilda *(1102-67)*
Daughter of Henry I

1485-1603
The Tudors

Mary *(1496-1533)*
Henry VIII's sister
Mary *(1516-58)*
Daughter of Henry VIII
Later Queen Mary I
Elizabeth *(1533-1603)*
Later Queen Elizabeth I
Daughter of Henry VIII

1603-1714
The Stuarts

Elizabeth *(1596-1662)*
Daughter of James I
Elizabeth *(1635-50)*
2nd daughter Charles I
Mary *(1662-94)*
Ist daughter of James II
Later Queen Mary II
Anne *(1665-1714)*
2nd daughter of James II
Later Queen Anne

Yuck! I like Princes best

Wow! wouldn't it be fun to be a princess

and rich too

1714-1901
The Hanoverians

Anne *(1709-59)*
Amelia *(1711-86)*
Caroline *(1713-57)*
Daughters of George II

Charlotte *(1766-1828)*
Augusta *(1768-1840)*
Elizabeth *(1770-1840)*
Mary *(1776-1857)*
Sophia *(1777-1848)*
Amelia *(1783-1810)*
Daughters of George III

Victoria *(1817-1901)*
Later Queen Victoria
Daughter of Edward,
Duke of Kent

1901-10
Saxe-Coburg-Gotha

Alexandra *of Denmark*
(1844-1925)
Wife of Edward VII

1910-
The Windsors

Elizabeth *(born 1926-)*
Later Queen Elizabeth II
1st daughter of George VI
Margaret *(1930-2002)*
2nd daughter of George VI
Anne *(born 1950-)*
Daughter of Elizabeth II
Diana *(1961-97)*
Princess of Wales
Daughter-in-law
of Elizabeth II
Beatrice *(born 1988-)*
Granddaughter of Elizabeth II

ooh! nice swords

Historic Royal
PALACES

Historic Royal Palaces is the independent charity that looks after the Tower of London, Hampton Court Palace, The Banqueting House, Kensington Palace and Kew Palace. We help everyone explore the story of how monarchs and people have shaped society, in some of the greatest palaces ever built.

We receive no funding from the Government or the Crown, so we depend on the support of our visitors, members, donors, volunteers and sponsors.

Published by Historic Royal Palaces
Hampton Court Palace
Surrey
KT8 9AU
© Historic Royal Palaces 2010

ISBN 978-1-873993-14-9

Text: *Elizabeth Newbery*
Design: *Rachel Hamdi and Iain Garrett*
Editors: *Sarah Kilby and Clare Murphy*
Picture Research: *Louise Nash*
Illustrations: *Tim Archbold*
Print: *City Digital Ltd*

Picture credits:

Abbreviations: b = bottom, c = centre, l = left, r = right, t = top

Front cover photograph: © Morley von Sternberg
© Board of Trustees of the Armouries: 19tr; By kind permission of the Trustees of the Chequers Estate / Mark Fiennes / The Bridgeman Art Library: 19cl; © Private Collection / The Bridgeman Art Library: 11cr, 17tl, 20tr; Private Collection/ © Look and Learn/ The Bridgeman Art Library: 20cl; © 2009 The British Library Board: 2tr; Camera Press: 15tl, 30bl; 4tr; © Hulton-Deutsch Collection/Corbis: 9t; © Stapleton Collection/Corbis: © English Heritage Photo Library: 21tr; © Getty Images: 9br, 9bl, 10l, 10c, 11cl, 22tr, 22br 23bl, 24cr: 29bl; © Roger-Viollet / Getty Images: 24tl; © Historic Royal Palaces: 6c, 14br, 27cl, 31r; © Historic Royal Palaces/Nick Guttridge: 2bl, 5tr, 6br, 16b, 18tr, 26tr; Mary Evans Picture Library: 14bc; © Mirrorpix: 32br, 33cl (detail); © Museum of London: 14tl, 21cl© Henry Grant Collection / Museum of London: 33cl; © National Maritime Museum: 28cl; ©National Portrait Gallery: 16cl: 16tr; © NTPL/David Garner: 31tl; © Rex Features: 3c, 23t, 29t, 32tl; Reuters: 25tr; The Royal Collection © 2009, Her Majesty Queen Elizabeth II: 4cr, 5cl, 6tl, 6tr, 7tr, 8cl, 8tr, 12l, 13tr, 13bl, 19tl, 23br, 26bl, 27tr 28tr, 29br, 30cr, 30tr; © Reserved/The Royal Collection: 8br; Society of Antiquaries, London: 18bl; © 2004 Topfoto: 3cl; © V&A Images : 12b, 12tr, 22tl, 25bl, 33tr; Wartski, London: 28br; © Zandra Rhodes: 10c.

Historic Royal Palaces is a registered charity (registered number 1068852)
www.hrp.org.uk